In the old age black was not counted fair, "Of His Lady Love." 1915
Charles Robinson

THE SONGS AND SONNETS OF WILLIAM SHAKESPEARE

ILLUSTRATED

ART BY ARTHUR RACKHAM, EDMUND DULAC,
CHARLES ROBINSON AND OTHERS

Selected and Edited by Jeff A. Menges

DOVER PUBLICATIONS, INC.
MINEOLA, NEW YORK

Copyright

Copyright © 2011 by Dover Publications, Inc.
Text copyright © 2011 by Jeff A. Menges
All rights reserved.

Bibliographical Note

This Dover edition, first published in 2011, is an original compilation of illustrations. The artists and sources include the following: John and Josiah Boydell, *The Dramatic Works of Shakespeare* (W. Bulmer and Company, London, 1802); John Gilbert, *The Plays of Shakespeare* (G. Routledge, London, 1858–61); Arthur Rackham, *A Midsummer Night's Dream* (Doubleday, Page & Co., New York, and William Heinemann, London, 1908); George Soper, *Tales from Shakespeare by Charles and Mary Lamb* (George Allen & Unwin Ltd., London, 1911); W. Heath Robinson, *Tales from Shakespeare by Charles Lamb* (Paisley/Alexander Gardner, London, 1909); Charles Folkard, *The Children's Shakespeare: Retold by Alice Spencer Hoffmann* (E. P. Dutton & Co., New York, and J. M. Dent & Sons, Ltd., London, 1911); Maud and Miska Petersham, *Tales from Shakespeare by Charles and Mary Lamb* (The Macmillan Company, New York, 1923); Walter Crane, *Flowers from Shakespeare's Garden Pictured by Walter Crane* (Cassell & Co., Ltd., London, 1906); Hugh Thomson, *The Merry Wives of Windsor* (Frederick A. Stokes Company, New York, 1910); Charles Robinson, *The Songs and Sonnets of William Shakespeare* (Duckworth & Co., London, n.d.); Artūs Scheiner, *Tales from Shakespeare by Charles and Mary Lamb* (The John C. Winston Company, Philadelphia, 1914); Norman M. Price, *Tales from Shakespeare by Charles and Mary Lamb* (Charles Scribner's Sons, New York, and T. C. and E. C. Jack, London, 1905 [?]); Walter Paget, *Tales from Shakespeare by Charles and Mary Lamb* (Ernest Nisler, London, and E. P. Dutton, New York, c. 1901); Frank C. Papé, *Tales from Shakespeare by Charles and Mary Lamb* (Frederick Warne & Co., Ltd., London and New York, 1923); Louis Rhead, *Tales from Shakespeare by Charles and Mary Lamb* (Harper & Brothers Publishers, New York and London, 1918); Arthur Rackham, *Tales from Shakespeare by Charles and Mary Lamb* (J. M. Dent & Co., London, and E. P. Dutton, New York, 1909); Matthew W. Peters, William Mulready, John Gilbert, William Hatherell, *Shakespeare in Pictorial Art* (John Lane Company, New York, 1916).

Library of Congress Cataloging-in-Publication Data

Shakespeare illustrated : art by Arthur Rackham, Edmund Dulac, Charles Robinson and others selected and edited by Jeff A. Menges. — Dover ed.
    p. cm.
  Compilation of illustrations by various artists from a number of sources.
  ISBN-13: 978-0-486-47890-6
  ISBN-10: 0-486-47890-4
   1. Shakespeare, William, 1564–1616—Illustrations. I. Menges, Jeff A. II. Title: Art by Arthur Rackham, Edmund Dulac, Charles Robinson and others.

PR2883.S353 2011
741.6'4—dc22

                             2011006737

Manufactured in the United States by Courier Corporation
47890401
www.doverpublications.com

ILLUSTRATED

ART BY ARTHUR RACKHAM, EDMUND DULAC,
CHARLES ROBINSON AND OTHERS

Introduction

The plays of Shakespeare have endured for over four centuries, and have inspired dramatic productions all over the world. Lines of dialogue from Shakespeare's works are still used in discussions today. The plays themselves are performed at all levels of dramatic quality; there exists no comparable peer. What is it about Shakespeare that fuels this level of dedication? What does his work give its audience that has allowed it to maintain popularity for over four hundred years?

In the late sixteenth and early seventeenth centuries, Shakespeare's works were being performed in the Globe and Rose theaters in London, where they enjoyed considerable popularity, even in his day. The houses filled to see his new works, with audiences ranging from the lowest would-be actors to members of the royal court. This was storytelling on a grand scale, with props and costumes transporting the crowd to another land, living lives that they could only dream of. They witnessed the love and honor that they longed for in their own lives, as well as the treachery and wickedness they were fortunate to avoid in their daily existence.

William Shakespeare's work is full of the human spirit—extremes of emotion laid bare—and history. There is often an involvement of the audience with the story, as if the secret that the characters share belongs to the audience as well. There are different levels of plot that intertwine, and, as in life, humor finds a place, even in the most dire and desperate circumstances.

Mark how one string, sweet husband to another, strikes each in each by mutual ordering, "Harmony and Melody." 1915
Charles Robinson
THE SONGS AND SONNETS OF WILLIAM SHAKESPEARE

Almost two centuries after Shakespeare's day, an undertaking wholly inspired by, and supporting, Shakespeare, began to take form. The project would take on a life of its own, producing a work that was, in its own right, quite remarkable for the time. In 1786, John Boydell, a London printer and engraver, conceived of producing a large illustrated edition of Shakespeare's works. The plan was grand in scope—there would need to be a large number of paintings commissioned, and those same images engraved; by the project's end, they numbered nearly 170. A gallery building was planned and constructed for the purpose of displaying the original works and selling folios of prints and bound volumes.

The project lasted over a decade, incurring both high praise and harsh criticism along its

The Merchant of Venice, Act III, Sc. I. 1864
John Gilbert

course. Boydell's intent was multi-faceted. He felt that such a project could form the basis of a national art identity for England, combining painters, engravers, and the passion for Shakespeare that the country held with pride. While it would most certainly have been more profitable to consider projects of a more modest undertaking, Boydell believed that this venture would nevertheless achieve his goals. The difficulty of managing a project so involved, considering production delays from engravers and a few negative reviews, did not stand in the way of Boydell's bringing the project to a close, producing a body of work that is still esteemed today for its detail, dedication, and depth of imagery.

The next opportunity to provide us with so much Shakespeare imagery was the brother-and-sister team of Charles and Mary Lamb. In 1807, just a few years after Boydell's venture, this pair of writers produced the volume *Tales from Shakespeare*. In it, they retold twenty of Shakespeare's works in language that was friendlier to the readers of the time. They took great care to preserve the words of the Bard where possible and to avoid modern phrasing. The book was immensely popular and was produced often in an illustrated edition—the earliest of which used images from Boydell's gallery.

Often considered a children's variant for its accessibility, the Lambs' *Tales from Shakespeare* continued to be reprinted well into the Golden Age of illustration, and many popular illustrators and publishers found that the public's appreciation for Shakespeare still made it an attractive subject for a richly illustrated edition.

Titania. 1911
George Soper
Tales from Shakespeare by Charles and Mary Lamb

Many of the plays received "gift book" treatments, for which numerous full-page illustrations accompanied the full text of the work, in an attractive case. These were often produced for release during the holiday period for gift giving. Arthur Rackham and Edmund Dulac were at the forefront of this publishing movement, and both have works represented here from such efforts. The Lambs' *Tales of*

Shakespeare became a staple in Victorian and Edwardian households, containing some very sophisticated works: the rich color paintings of Norman M. Price, Frank Papé's complex line work, and Louis Rhead's ink drawings, ranging from simple vignettes to scenes crowded with layers of finely rendered figures.

By the late nineteenth century, the ageless quality of Shakespeare's tales was widely recognized. In an empire that was looking to uphold its cultural icons, Shakespeare became embraced as a symbol of British excellence. The stories, apart from the stage, were also well known, and were very popular with all levels of society. The acceptance of Shakespeare's work on a higher social level made it a respected subject for gallery works, attracting artists who aren't perceived as illustrators, such as John Everett Millais, John Singer Sargent, and John William Waterhouse. Shakespeare's themes also translated well to the thinking of the pre-Raphaelite artists.

In the pages and on the illustration plates that follow are remarkably inspired graphic works by some of the greatest artists and illustrators of their day. The costumes and customs of Shakespeare's period made for interesting visual subjects. In a few of the plays, the realm of the supernatural plays a part; acts of magic and the creatures that dwell with it provide an opportunity for the artist to stretch the imagination. During a period when fairy painting was an art movement in fine-art circles, characters such as Puck, Titania, and Ariel provided serious subject matter with literary clout.

It is our hope that the continued appreciation of Shakespeare will find this new collection of images, ranging from eighteenth-century painting to the height of illustration's Golden Age, a welcome assembly of visual information for the admirer of Shakespeare's stories, the lover of the theater, and the artist who seeks both reference and inspiration.

Jeff A. Menges
October 2010

In the Court of Love, "Soul and Body." 1915
Charles Robinson

THE SONGS AND SONNETS OF WILLIAM SHAKESPEARE

FEATURED PLAYS

The art selected is from a variety of sources, indicated on each plate.

The plays appear in the approximate order in which they were written (actual dates are unobtainable in many cases).

INDEX OF ARTISTS

THE PLATES

"Enter OPHELIA,
  fantastically dressed with straws and flowers."

Romeo and Juliet

Perhaps Shakespeare's best-known and best-loved play, *Romeo and Juliet* was written and produced very early in the Bard's career. The tale is one of forbidden love—two warring families in Verona, Italy, are filled with a deep hatred for each other older than their understanding of its origins. A pair of ill-fated teens meet at a masquerade and fall deeply in love, only to find that they belong to their family's rival clan. Their story is a tragic one, woven with unfortunate timing and fallen comrades, as well as the ultimate sacrifice, when life without the other appears to be the future.

The most memorable scene in *Romeo and Juliet* is that of Juliet on her chamber balcony calling into the night for her newly met love, not knowing he is in the brambles below. He climbs up the trellis to steal an embrace, leading to one of the greatest scenes romantic literature has ever provided, and one that has been painted repeatedly in attempts to capture its passion.

The Reconciliation of the Montagues and Capulets over the Dead Bodies of Romeo and Juliet. 1853–5. Frederic, Lord Leighton

Act III. Sc. 5.

Title page. Act III, Sc. V. c.1860
John Gilbert

ROMEO AND JULIET

Romeo and Juliet. 1870
Ford Madox Brown

ROMEO AND JULIET

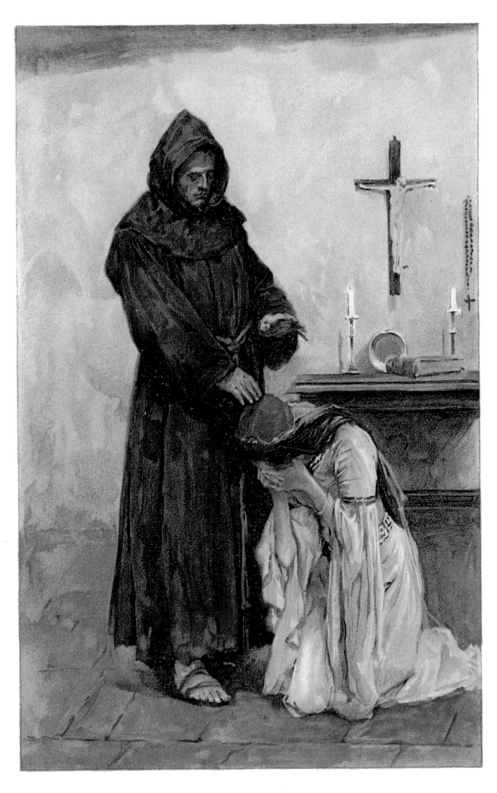

Juliet applied to the friendly friar. 1901
Walter Paget

ROMEO AND JULIET

Romeo and Juliet. Act V, Sc. III. c. 1905

Norman M. Price

ROMEO AND JULIET

Romeo whispered that he must be gone. 1911
Charles Folkard

ROMEO AND JULIET

"O Romeo, Romeo! Wherefore art thou Romeo?" 1912
William Hatherell, R. I.

ROMEO AND JULIET

Here Romeo took his last leave of his lady's lips. 1914
Artŭs Scheiner

ROMEO AND JULIET

The day was breaking when they parted. 1923
Frank C. Papé

ROMEO AND JULIET

Valentine Rescuing Sylvia from Proteus, 1851. William Holman Hunt

The Two Gentlemen of Verona
c. 1592–3

Portrayed in this tale of two friends, their loves, and the intertwined roads they travel is the comparison and contrast of their romantic love to their friendship. When one gets in the way of the other, there are prices paid, and all bonds are tested. This is one of Shakespeare's earliest plays, featuring female leads dressed as men as a form of disguise. This becomes an oft-repeated device in Shakespeare's works—one that adds to the complexity of the story and the confusion of the characters, but may allow for personal confessions to be made in the presence of the intended and true feelings to be shared.

This comedy ends lightly, but not without treading upon a few social standards, especially when viewed in light of today's balances of male–female relationships, making aspects of *Two Gentlemen of Verona* subject to some modern criticisms that the play did not endure when it was written.

JULIA: *O good sir, my master charged me to deliver a ring to Madam Silvia,*
which, out of my neglect, was never done." 1802
John and Josiah Boydell

THE TWO GENTLEMEN OF VERONA

THE
TWO GENTLEMEN of VERONA.

Page 33.

Title page. Act IV, Sc. IV. c. 1860
John Gilbert

THE TWO GENTLEMEN OF VERONA

Valentine, having heard his robbers had taken a lady prisoner,
came to console and relieve her. 1911
George Soper

THE TWO GENTLEMEN OF VERONA

He was all at once seized with penitence and remorse. 1914
Artůs Scheiner

THE TWO GENTLEMEN OF VERONA

She beheld her lover serenading the Lady Silvia with music. 1918
Louis Rhead

THE TWO GENTLEMEN OF VERONA

Valentine came to console and relieve her. 1923
Frank C. Papé

THE TWO GENTLEMEN OF VERONA

A Midsummer Night's Dream
c. 1594–95

Visually, this play is likely the richest of all of Shakespeare's works. Its cast of fairies and fantastic characters set in a magical wood make this a play that has an extremely broad appeal to artists as well as audiences. It is not surprising, then, that we find more illustrated forms of *A Midsummer Night's Dream* than any other Shakespeare play. To this day it remains one of his most frequently performed works.

Among these illustrations, the image of Titania—the beautiful queen of the fairies—has long had an appeal to the artist. Her image was especially popular during the Victorian era of fairy painting in the late nineteenth century.

Two extraordinary illustrated editions of *A Midsummer Night's Dream* were produced in the early twentieth century: one with William Heath Robinson's illustrations, which is a treatise in line work, and, just a few years earlier, another with the beautiful color imagery of Arthur Rackham. Both volumes are highly sought after by collectors and fans of the play, and the art.

The Quarrel of Oberon and Titania. 1849. Joseph Noel Paton

Hermia and the Fairies. 1861
John Simmons

A Midsummer Night's Dream

Titania's Awakening. 1896
Charles Sims

A Midsummer Night's Dream

OBERON: *"What thou seest when thou dost wake,*
Do it for thy true-love take." 1901
Walter Paget

A MIDSUMMER NIGHT'S DREAM

. . . the moon, like to a silver bow New bent in heaven. 1908
Arthur Rackham

A MIDSUMMER NIGHT'S DREAM

Come, now a roundel. 1908
Arthur Rackham

A MIDSUMMER NIGHT'S DREAM

One aloof stand sentinel. 1908
Arthur Rackham

A MIDSUMMER NIGHT'S DREAM

I will sing, that they shall hear I am not afraid. 1908
Arthur Rackham

A MIDSUMMER NIGHT'S DREAM

Never so weary, never so in woe. 1908
Arthur Rackham

A MIDSUMMER NIGHT'S DREAM

. . . Are you sure That we are awake?
It seems to me That yet we sleep, we dream. 1908
Arthur Rackham

A MIDSUMMER NIGHT'S DREAM

Titania Sleeps. Act II, Sc. II. 1905
Norman M. Price

A MIDSUMMER NIGHT'S DREAM

LYSANDER: . . . *and she, sweet lady, sweet lady, dotes, Devoutly dotes in idolatry,*
Upon this spotted and inconstant man. 1914
W. Heath Robinson

A MIDSUMMER NIGHT'S DREAM

PUCK: *How now, spirit! whither wander you?* 1914
W. Heath Robinson

A MIDSUMMER NIGHT'S DREAM

Titania: *Playing on pipes of corn, and versing love to amorous Phillida.* 1914
W. Heath Robinson

A Midsummer Night's Dream

TITANIA: *To dance our ringlets to the whistling wind.* 1914
W. Heath Robinson

A MIDSUMMER NIGHT'S DREAM

HELENA: *O weary night, O long and tedious night.* 1914
W. Heath Robinson

A MIDSUMMER NIGHT'S DREAM

TITANIA: *"Be kind and courteous to this gentleman."* Act III, Sc. I. 1914
W. Heath Robinson

A MIDSUMMER NIGHT'S DREAM

The Merchant of Venice

c. 1596

The Venetian merchant Antonio becomes an unwitting victim in one of Shakespeare's best-known plays. In securing a loan to enable his close friend Bassanio to pursue a dream of love, the merchant is asked to sign an unusual bond with potentially tragic results, if the debt cannot be repaid in time. Feeling secure in this, he agrees with little hesitation. When things go awry and the bond comes due, it is Bassanio—or more so—his newly found bride Portia, who, in the guise of an incredibly crafty lawyer, comes to the rescue of the merchant Antonio, who helped make their union possible.

The moneylender in the story is the character Shylock, traditionally portrayed as a villain, but in recent times regarded with sympathy as a character in search of his dignity. The hard line that Shylock takes on the payment of the bond becomes his undoing in the end. Shylock remains the most identifiable character in *The Merchant of Venice,* and is the most-often depicted figure from the play.

A Despatch from Trezibond, 1873. Henry Wallis

SHYLOCK: *I'll have my bond; I will not hear thee speak: I'll have my bond;*
and therefore speak no more. Act III, Sc. III. 1802
John and Josiah Boydell

THE MERCHANT OF VENICE

Act IV. Sc. 1.

Title page. Act IV, Sc. I. c. 1860
John Gilbert

THE MERCHANT OF VENICE

"O noble judge! O excellent young man!" 1911
Charles Folkard

THE MERCHANT OF VENICE

"Why then, Antonio," said Portia, *"You must prepare your bosom for the knife."* 1914
Artŭs Scheiner

THE MERCHANT OF VENICE

"Tarry a little, Jew," said Portia, "This bond here gives you no drop of blood." 1918
Louis Rhead

THE MERCHANT OF VENICE

"This bond here gives you no drop of blood" 1923
Frank C. Papé

THE MERCHANT OF VENICE

As You Like It

c. 1599

Exiled from the lands of her birth by a wicked uncle, Rosalind, daughter of the rightful Duke, and her constant companion and cousin Celia (the wicked Duke's daughter), take refuge in disguise and find a fair and quiet existence in the forest of Arden. When Fate should bring their way a fellow whom Rosalind had fallen for while at the Duke's court, the heroine finds herself in a situation much to her pleasing, able to survey her suitor's feelings from a lofty perch by means of her new and deceptive identity.

There is a complex web of loves and proposals among the exiled, the courtiers, and the native people of the forest of Arden, yet everything is realigned when the true identities are revealed. There are no fewer than four weddings in the end; the exiled are forgiven, and the wicked have repented.

As You like It remains one of Shakespeare's more popular works, and is the source of the famous quote: "All the world's a stage."

The Seven Ages. Act II, Sc. VII. 1838. William Mulready, R. A.

A Scene from "As You Like It." 1853
Walter Howell Deverell

AS YOU LIKE IT

GANIMED: *I will feign myself to be Rosalind, and you shall feign to court me."* 1901
Walter Paget

AS YOU LIKE IT

Rosalind and Celia in the Forest of Arden. Act II, Sc. IV. 1905
Norman M. Price

As You Like It

Come, have a good heart, my sister Aliena. 1909
W. Heath Robinson

As You Like It

"I care not for my spirits if my legs were not weary." 1911
Charles Folkard

As You Like It

Oliver, Rosalind, and Celia. 1914
Artŭs Scheiner

AS YOU LIKE IT

Ophelia, 1852. Sir John Everett Millais

Hamlet

c. 1599

Some of Shakespeare's most memorable scenes and oft-repeated lines originate in this play, which is certainly among his best known. *Hamlet* is the tale of a young prince of Denmark who suffers the loss of his father, the king. The king's ghost appears and relays to the prince that, in truth, his own brother — young Hamlet's uncle, who now sits upon the throne — indeed killed the king — and the ghost demands to be avenged.

The play is largely about the inner turmoil that the title character faces in the knowledge the ghost has delivered, which is compounded when the uncle takes not only the throne, but the company of Hamlet's mother, the queen, as well. The dismay and confusion that fill Hamlet not only drive him to the brink, but affects those around him as well, including his fair lady Ophelia.

The image of Lady Ophelia, who drowned in shallow waters, became immensely popular as a painting subject in Victorian England. Not found in illustration alone, but also on large canvases in galleries, it was a staple of the Pre-Raphaelite's portfolio, including this most famous rendition by Sir John Everett Millais.

Hamlet and Horatio in the Graveyard. 1839
Eugène Delacroix

HAMLET

Ophelia (by the pond). 1894
John William Waterhouse

HAMLET

"There's rosemary, that's for remembrance;

"There's rosemary, that's for remembrance." 1906
Walter Crane

HAMLET

The Ghost solemnly beckoned him on. 1911
Charles Folkard

HAMLET

HAMLET

Opening page. 1922
John Austen

HAMLET

Act I, Sc. V. 1922
John Austen

Hamlet

Act III, Sc. IV. 1922
John Austen

HAMLET

Act IV, Sc. VII. 1922

John Austen

HAMLET

Act V, Sc. I. 1922
John Austen

HAMLET

To this brook she came one day. 1923
Frank C. Papé

HAMLET

The Merry Wives of Windsor
c. 1597-99

This comedy play features a character who won great praise in Shakespeare's day, that of Sir John Falstaff. Falstaff's popularity was such that the Bard wrote him into this contemporary work. Previously the character had existed in the fifteenth-century story of *Henry IV, Part 1*. In this tale our knight finds himself at Windsor in a dire financial situation and devises a scheme to regain his status: he will court a pair of wealthy, *married* women—thus the play's title—in hopes of sharing in their wealth, or, if necessary, blackmailing them.

When the wives, Mistress Page and Mistress Ford, mutually discover Falstaff's deceit, they decide to turn the tables on the charlatan by playing into his ruse and put him through his paces at the expense of his dignity. As a subplot, there are a number of suitors vying for the hand of Mistress Page's daughter, Anne. The two storylines cross in the later scenes, in which there is orchestrated confusion, creating the opportunity for everything to fall into its proper place.

Falstaff in the Buckbasket. 1792. Henry Fuseli

MRS. FORD: *Sir John! art thou there, my deer? my male deer?*
Act V, Sc. V. 1802
John and Josiah Boydell

THE MERRY WIVES OF WINDSOR

Act I. Sc. 1.

Title page. Act I, Sc. I. c. 1860
John Gilbert

THE MERRY WIVES OF WINDSOR

"Let's consult together against this greasy knight." 1910
Hugh Thomson

The Merry Wives of Windsor

"If he were twenty Sir John Falstaffs, he shall not abuse
Robert Shallow, Esquire!" 1910
Hugh Thomson

The Merry Wives of Windsor

"Enter Anne Page with wine, Mistress Ford and Mistress Page following." 1910
Hugh Thomson

THE MERRY WIVES OF WINDSOR

"They cover him with foul linen." 1910
Hugh Thomson

THE MERRY WIVES OF WINDSOR

Much Ado About Nothing

This comedy looks at the diversity of love, provided by two couples who present their romances as contrasting models. Two friends and fellow officers returning from a battle, Claudio and Benedick, each have relationships in Messina. Claudio's love for Hero is one of deep emotion, so much so that the couple is often without words for the feelings they have for each other. Benedick's love is for Beatrice, a girl who at first seems to thrive on heated banter with Benedick, until they both realize that their appreciation of the other's wit is a draw to them both.

The friction in the story is created by the meddling of Don John, the brother to the lord whom Claudio and Benedick serve. In an attempt to gain revenge against his half-brother, Don Pedro, Don John plants a lie with Claudio—hoping to anger him against Don Pedro. The plan nearly succeeds—but it is not the end of Don John's plots—and the resulting twists and complications almost divide the two pairs of lovers.

" Get you some of this distilled Carduus Benedictus and lay it to your heart; — "
" Why Benedictus? You have some moral in this Benedictus "
" Moral? No, by my troth. I have no moral meaning; I meant, plain Holy thistle "

Much Ado about Nothing. Act iii., Sc. 4.

"Moral? No, by my troth. I have no moral meaning: I meant, plain Holy thistle." Act III, Sc. IV. 1906. Walter Crane

Hero, Ursula and Beatrice. Act III, Sc. I. 1790
Rev. Matthew W. Peters, R. A.

MUCH ADO ABOUT NOTHING

Act IV. Sc. 1.

Title Page. Act IV, Sc. I. c. 1860
John Gilbert

MUCH ADO ABOUT NOTHING

Beatrice and Benedick. Act IV, Sc. 1. 1905
Norman M. Price

MUCH ADO ABOUT NOTHING

"I will live in thy heart, die in thy lap, and be buried in thy eyes." 1911
Charles Folkard

MUCH ADO ABOUT NOTHING

He swore to Beatrice that he took her but for pity. 1914
Artŭs Scheiner

MUCH ADO ABOUT NOTHING

They saw Borachio standing under the window. 1923
Frank C. Papé

MUCH ADO ABOUT NOTHING

Twelfth Night

c. 1599–1601

In Shakespeare's England, "Twelfth Night" referred to the twelfth night after Christmas day—it is believed that this play was written with that celebration in mind. The rituals had elements that would greatly appeal to Shakespeare's storytelling—including dressing as someone or something other than yourself, which was one of Shakespeare's favorite devices.

The story is set in Illyria, on the eastern coast of the Adriatic Sea. After a shipwreck, Viola is convinced that her twin brother Sebastian was killed in the mishap. She seeks to ease her own pain by serving the Duke Orsino—but in seeking employment disguises herself as a man. The Duke takes on this new page, called "Cesario," and uses "him" as a messenger to carry news of his love to the fair Lady Olivia. Viola falls in love with the Duke, and Lady Olivia falls in love with Cesario. The plot becomes more complex when Viola's twin brother—who survived the shipwreck—enters the mix, and adds the element of a mistaken identity to Viola's disguise.

Act II, Sc. IV. 1850. Walter Howell Deverell

OLIVIA: *Now go with me and with this holy man/Into the chantry by.*
Act IV, Sc. III. 1802
John and Josiah Boydell

TWELFTH NIGHT

Title Page. Act III, Sc. IV. c. 1860
John Gilbert

TWELFTH NIGHT

"I will draw the curtain and show the picture." 1901
Walter Paget

TWELFTH NIGHT

OLIVIA: *"But we will draw the curtain and show you the picture."*
Act I, Sc. V. 1905
Norman M. Price

TWELFTH NIGHT

Sir Toby held the youth roughly. 1911
Charles Folkard

TWELFTH NIGHT

She began to think of confessing that she was a woman. 1923
Frank C. Papé

TWELFTH NIGHT

King Lear, 1898. Edwin Austin Abbey

King Lear

c. 1605

This is a story of an aged king approaching the end of his days—and the division of his lands and worldly goods among his three daughters, Goneril, Regan, and Cordelia. King Lear seeks to find the daughter who loves him the best, upon whom he will bestow the greatest part of his kingdom, and asks his daughters for an admission of their love for him. Goneril and Regan both rise to the part, saying the right things to gain their father's favor, while Cordelia, in her simple honesty, does not embellish her feelings.

This is a truly tragic tale in which the dying king learns of the mistakes in his judgment—of the lies his daughters tell him for their own benefit, and his inability to see the truer heart of Cordelia—leading to painful repercussions that escort him to his very end.

Based on a tale of an ancient Celtic king, the costume and court presence of this play might resemble some Arthurian age, giving it an unusually strong appeal to a romantic artist, as shown in this scene painted by Edwin Austin Abbey in 1898.

CORDELIA: *I know you what you are; And like a sister am most loath to call*
Your faults as they are nam'd. Love well our father. Act I, Sc. I. 1802
John and Josiah Boydell

KING LEAR

Title Page. Act V, Sc. III. c. 1860
John Gilbert

King Lear

LEAR: *"Cordelia, Cordelia."* Act V, Sc. III. 1905
Norman M. Price

KING LEAR

Cordelia. 1909
Arthur Rackham

KING LEAR

Only the Fool was with him. 1911
Charles Folkard

KING LEAR

A tender sight it was to see the meeting between
this father and daughter. 1914
Artŭs Scheiner

KING LEAR

"Howl, Howl, Howl, Howl! O, You are men of stones." 1918
Louis Rhead

KING LEAR

A tender sight it was to see the meeting between this father and daughter. 1923
Frank C. Papé

King Lear

Macbeth

One of the better known of Shakespeare's tragedies, this play presents an interesting group of image-inspiring characters. Macbeth, a Scottish general, encounters three witches and hears their prophecy: He will became Thane of Cawdor and then king of Scotland. After first dismissing their predictions, Macbeth begins to believe in the witches' vision. He sets his ambitions on becoming king.

With Lady Macbeth conspiring alongside him, a plan is conceived and executed to help move Macbeth to the throne, but the difficulty in maintaining it, as well as haunting visits from the ghosts of the slain, torture the usurper. The lords around Macbeth grow increasingly suspicious and distrustful. Macbeth attempts to avoid the witches' final prophecy, his loss of the throne, but the prophecy is realized after his loss in battle to the Scottish Thane Macduff.

With powerful figures and elements of the supernatural winding through the tale, *Macbeth* remains one of the strongest visual plays in Shakespeare's canon.

Macbeth, Act III, Sc. I. John Gilbert

Macbeth Consulting the Vision of the Armed Head. 1794
Henry Fuseli

MACBETH

MACBETH: *[Seeing Ghost.] Avaunt! And quit my sight!*
let the earth hide thee! Act III, Sc. IV. 1802
John and Josiah Boydell

MACBETH

Ellen Terry as Lady Macbeth. 1889
John Singer Sargent

MACBETH

The Weird Sisters. Act IV, Sc. I. 1905
Norman M. Price

Macbeth

Three forms, wild and unearthly. 1911
Charles Folkard

MACBETH

"Macbeth, beware of Macduff, The Thane of Fife." 1918
Louis Rhead

Macbeth

Frontispiece for *Tales from Shakespeare*. 1918
Frank Schoonover

MACBETH

They were stopped by the strange appearance of three figures. 1923
Frank C. Papé

MACBETH

The Tempest

Shakespeare's *The Tempest* runs a close second to *A Midsummer Night's Dream* as a story that has captured the imaginative efforts of artists and illustrators. The storm itself provides fodder for imagery, as well as the resulting shipwreck and the setting of the story on a remote island. The island is the home of Prospero, the exiled rightful Duke of Milan, his daughter Miranda, and a beastly wretch born of a witch—Prospero's slave Caliban.

As in *A Midsummer Night's Dream*, the landscape of *The Tempest* is also populated by magical characters from the realm of fairie, adding to the potential for imaginative visuals. The character of Ariel, an air spirit, was quite a popular painting subject in Victorian circles.

Prospero's confinement has given him the great opportunity for study and learning, transforming him into something of a wizard. When a ship carrying Prospero's brother, and some of the conspirators who placed him on the island many years before, passes within range, Prospero raises *The Tempest* to wreck their ship and then deals with them accordingly, steering their fate as each group of castaways wanders the island.

Miranda—The Tempest. 1916. John William Waterhouse

Ferdinand and Miranda Playing Chess. 1871
Lucy Madox Brown

THE TEMPEST

Miranda: *"Sweet lord, you play me false."*
Ferdinand: *"No my dearest love I would not for the world."* Act V, Sc. I. 1893.
Walter Crane

The Tempest

"CERES, most bounteous lady, thy rich lees
Of wheat, rye, barley,"
                                    Tempest, Act iv, Sc. 1.

"Ceres, most bounteous lady, thy rich lees of wheat, rye, barley,"
Act IV, Sc. I. 1906.
Walter Crane

THE TEMPEST

112

PROSPERO: *"What seest thou else in the dark backward and abysm of time?"*
Act I, Sc. II. 1908
Edmund Dulac

THE TEMPEST

PROSPERO: *"And to my state grew stranger, being transported and rapt in secret studies,"* Act I, Sc. II. 1908
Edmund Dulac

THE TEMPEST

PROSPERO: *"She did confine thee . . . and in her most unmitigable rage,
into a cloven pine."* Act I, Sc. II. 1908
Edmund Dulac

THE TEMPEST

CALIBAN: *"Sounds and sweet airs, that give delight and hurt not."*
Act III, Sc. II. 1908
Edmund Dulac

THE TEMPEST

Miranda: *"Sweet lord, you play me false."* Act V, Sc. I. 1908
Edmund Dulac

The Tempest

The feast vanished away. Act III, Sc. III. 1905
Norman M. Price

THE TEMPEST

*He took rather too much pleasure in tormenting
an ugly monster called Caliban.* 1923
Frank C. Papé

The Tempest

The Tempest. 1923
Maud and Miska Petersham

The Tempest

ARIEL: *Hark, hark!* Act I, Sc. II. 1926
Arthur Rackham

THE TEMPEST

I'll kiss thy foot: I'll swear myself thy subject. Act II, Sc. II. 1926

Arthur Rackham

THE TEMPEST

*The isle is full of noises, Sounds and sweet airs, that give delight
and hurt not.* Act III, Sc. II. 1926
Arthur Rackham

THE TEMPEST

Sometimes a thousand twangling instruments
Will hum about mine ears. Act III, Sc. II. 1926
Arthur Rackham

THE TEMPEST

Go charge my goblins that they grind their joints
With dry convulsions. Act IV, Sc. I. 1926
Arthur Rackham

THE TEMPEST